The Law of FAITH

Mark II: 22-26

MAURICE J. LITZOW

Ark House Press
arkhousepress.com

Cataloguing in Publication Data:
Title: The Law of Faith | ISBN: 978-1-7645620-3-4 (pbk)
Subjects: REL006700 RELIGION / Biblical Studies / Bible Study Guides; REL077000 RELIGION / Faith; REL012120 RELIGION / Christian Living / Spiritual Growth.

Design by initiateagency.com

CONTENTS

INTRODUCTION

How this book came into being, at the time I started this writing I was living in Japan. I was listening to a Kenneth Hagin podcast about Mark 11:23. I wanted to read along with this message so I opened my bible to Mark 11:22 and as soon as I did the Spirit of God leapt up inside me and said, "I want you to write about this scripture." In my mind I thought he wants me to study this scripture and he knows me well, He knows, for me to learn, I need to write it out.

So I started to write and write and write. It surprised me what came out of me, as I heard it, I wrote it.

I soon realised this is becoming more than study notes but it was taking shape as a book. I asked God, "why do you want me to write this, as it is a well preached and written about scripture, by some very anointed preachers." He said to me, "There are many people who want to know about Mark 11:22-26 but these people 'slip through the cracks'." The people that others do not reach. The way you write will catch their attention and give them understanding."

I was very surprised at this, as in my earlier life I was never known to be a writer of any type.

I guess my point is regardless of your self image, if God asks you to do something there is a purpose to get a blessing to someone. Possibly only you, but I doubt that but a blessing for many. Everything God does is for the benefit of people.

Be encouraged when God sets you a task it is always bigger than you but He wants it done and He supplies the equipment, tools, ideas, finances etc. to get it done. It will *save* lives and it will *change* lives.

Chapter ONE

MARK 11: 22-26 NKJV

So Jesus answered and said to them,"Have faith in God. For assuredly, I say to you, whoever says to this mountain, 'Be removed and be cast into the sea,' and does not doubt in his heart, but believes that those things he says will be done, he will have whatever he says. Therefore I say to you, whatever things you ask when you pray, believe that you receive them,and you will have them. "And whenever you stand praying,if you have anything against anyone, forgive him, that your Father in heaven may also forgive you your trespasses. But if you do not forgive, neither will your Father in heaven forgive your trespasses."

This teaching and explanation by Jesus was in response to Peters statement in verse 21 *"And Peter, remembering, said to him "Rabbi look! The fig tree which you cursed has withered away."* NKJV

The fig tree back story

The back story of this teaching is found in Mark11: 12-14, we will see why Peter responded with amazement at the withered fig tree.

Jesus came out of a town called Bethany and was hungry so he was looking for something to eat and he saw this fig tree from a distance, and was hopeful of eating. He soon found that this fig tree was void of fruit. It had leaves on it so it looked like a fig tree, appeared to act like a fig tree (because it had leaves and gave the appearance of fruit bearing) but produced no fruit. The fact is it really was a fig tree but had become useless, you would think that the main purpose of a fig tree was to produce fruit, namely figs. These figs are purposed to give sustenance to people, remember that everything God does is for the benefit of people. If it is not doing what its intended purpose then it should be replaced, with a tree that will do as it was commanded to do from the beginning of time.

There are a number messages on what the fig tree represents but I will leave that to others at this time, as that is not the purpose of this writing.

As we read in verse 14, Jesus spoke to the fruitless fig tree saying: *"Let no one eat fruit from you ever again."* NKJV

This is the last words the disciples heard from Jesus regarding the fig tree, and by the biblical accounts Jesus did not give it another thought. He went about his business.

Why is it that Jesus went about his business and didn't give the fig tree incident another thought?

Jesus had faith in God and he understood how faith works, he used it and he had total confidence in the words he spoke.

I also ask myself why did Peter get so excited about the demise of the fig tree?

He had been hanging out with Jesus, you would think this is normal but Peter, like us was sort of new at how faith works and the power it contains, seems as though he had not seen anything like this in his life and was in amazement at the outcome. He was amazed at the Faith filled words of Jesus and what it achieved.

I can imagine him saying to himself, "What!" Again he did that with just words, first was the casting out of demons, then the leper healed, then again the paralytic, not only that he restored withered hands and calms the storm with his words."

There must be something that words contain that will create change.

Why curse the poor fig tree?

This seems so out of character of Jesus, for he went about preaching the good news of salvation but the poor fig tree.

There are some great writings on the symbolism of the death of the fig tree. It is said to be symbolic of judgement, of empty religion. I want to bring into our attention who Jesus is and by what authority did he have to speak these words to the fig tree.

As we see in scripture Jesus was the only begotten Son of God (John 3; 16), he is the first born from the dead (Rom. 8: 29), In Him is the light and life of Man (John 1: 4), Alpha and Omega (Rev. 22: 13) and many more but most of all he is The Word of God (John 1; 1, Rev. 19:13).

Through him was all things were made and with out him nothing was made (John 1: 3).

God through Him created everything, including the fig tree. He is Lord over all of creation for through him all of it was created. Don't feel sorry for the fig tree, it was not doing what it was created to do and that is to produce figs. Basically The fig tree was telling Jesus, I refuse to do as I was instructed from the beginning, so Jesus being the Word, that was instrumental in creating all things, had the authority to speak to the rebellious fig tree.

Don't feel sorry for the fig tree.

Back to the main event

We return to the book of Mark, in verse 20 in NKJV, *"Now in the morning. As they passed by, they saw the fig tree dried up from its roots."* Seeing this is what caused Peter, in verse 21, to say *"Rabbi look! The fig tree which you cursed has withered away."* he said this in amazement. This gave Jesus the opportunity to reveal how Faith works.

Jesus said *"Have faith in God." vs 22.* In the following verses 23 to 26, he explains how the faith of God or *in* God works.

If we as believers followed this method exactly as Jesus describes then we would have 100% results, 100% of the time but I know few to many people who never see any results. They become frustrated and questioning, this is the exact door Satan wants left open.

He wants the believer to be ignorant and in dispute, deception is his only power, don't enter into the lies of our enemy.

I would like to explore what is meant by "*Have faith in God*", I am not sure if you have notices in church circles many can quote scripture but have no idea what it means, or how to operate it but they can quote it. It is possible that the word of God, the incorruptible seed that causes such great things to happen, gets lodged in the memory and doesn't make its way to its intended destination, this destination is the very heart of man.

Just a quick note for those who are upset with the term "man". Man is a created species of being, there is male man and female man. (Gen. 1: 27).

We want to do more than just quote it we want the Word of God manifesting and alive in us, and doing what it was intended to do and that is: to not be void but prosper to where God sent it. (Is. 55: 11)

We want to get the full understanding and revelation of Gods word, that is the full revelation of Jesus the Christ.

The manifestation of Jesus in this world is the most important and powerful thing to happen to mankind. The most pivotal point in the history of the world.

Remembering that God's grace and truth came to us through the Word of God, Jesus Christ. (John 1: 17)

Nothing else since the creation of all things has had so much impact on the world than the coming of Jesus the Christ.

Jesus cannot Lie

Jesus' opening response to Peters statement in verse 21 *"And Peter, remembering, said to him "Rabbi look! The fig tree which you cursed has withered away."* was *"Have faith in God"* verse 22.

For Jesus to respond in such a manner must mean that *"faith in God"* is available to those who believe it, and choose to use it. The results of which are seen in the fig tree and many other miracles recorded.

Jesus being The Word of God (John 1:1), God the Son (Luke 1:35), In Him the dwells fullness of the Godhead bodily (Colossians 2: 9) is the same as Father God, same character, same integrity and it is impossible for God, Jesus, the Holy Spirit to lie.

Numbers 23:19 says, *"**God is not a man, that He should lie, Nor a son of man**, that He should repent. Has He said, and will He not do? Or has He spoken, and will He not make it good?"* NKJV

Titus 1:2 says, *"In hope of eternal life which **God, who cannot lie,** promised before time began."* NKJV

Hebrews 6:18 says, *"That by two immutable things, **in which it is impossible for God to lie**...... "* NKJV

We are led to believe that nothing is impossible for God (Luke 1: 3) but I am thankful the only thing impossible for God is to lie.

Having discovered the integrity of God and his word, that there is no lies in Him, We can have confidence that his word is the total truth and sent to us for our benefit.

So when Jesus makes this statement "*have faith in God*" then it has to be true and it has to be available for us to use. It must to be

100% truth because there is no lies in God. There is no shadow of turning (James 1:7).

This scripture refers to how consistent God is, he is the Father of light no darkness at all in him. He remains unchanging therefore if he says *"have faith in God"* to a people who were still under Old Covenant values and as yet are not spiritually reborn, how much more are we able to work and have access to this faith.

How much more should we see all of the mountains that surround us be removed, it is possible for the things that Jesus said to be realised in the life of the believer? If it were not so God would be a liar but we know this is not the truth, he is the ultimate truth, the highest reality.

Everything he says is for our benefit and is available for us to use and have total provision for our lives.

So folks lets us put away every thought, offence, unforgiveness or the such like that would hinder us from acting as Jesus said and hinder us from getting the results promised.

Chapter TWO

HAVE FAITH IN GOD

This statement is a true statement, "*Have faith in God,*" if it wasn't the truth then Jesus would not have spoken it. It is easy to say, easy to quote but do we understand it?

This is my understanding of this statement: The method of operation that Jesus used was faith and this faith is of God, the faith Jesus was using was God's faith, Jesus is about to explain how Gods faith works, and it works every time. This Faith that is of God is available to us and God wants you to us it.

If he did not want you to know about it and use it, then Jesus would not give a tutorial on it. It pleases God when we live by the faith of God.

If we grasp this teaching we will be able to accomplish all things, Gods way.

How do we grasp this? Meditate on it until you see it and it will be a revelation to you. Then act on it. Faith is action. (Heb.11:1)

If we look into different versions of the bible, we will hopefully gain more understanding of verse 22, there are three consistent factors: you, faith and God. Let us take a look.

King James version, New King James version Amplified, NIV and many others say "*Have faith in God*" inferring that "*you*" Have faith in God.

In some of the literal translations:

The Literal Standard Version says, *"And Jesus answering says to them, "Have faith from God."*

Berean Literal Bible says, "*And Jesus answering, says to them, "Have faith from God."*

Young's Literal translation says,"*And Jesus answering saith to them, 'Have faith of God*"

Smith's Literal translation says, "*And Jesus having answered, says to them, Have the faith of God.*"

The Passion Translation says, *"Let the faith of God be in you"*

Just a disclaimer here: At his point I researched the Greek and Aramaic bibles and studies, but I'm not an Aramaic, Greek or Hebrew scholar. I understand from what I read that the Passion Translation was the most accurate. But that is my own personal study and there seems to be debate about these things, as always, so do your own research and gain more personal understanding.

Please note that from what I read, Jesus spoke Aramaic but the book of Mark was written in Greek.

Perhaps because Mark's audience were not Aramaic speakers but Greek speakers. Mark was possibly written between 50- 70 AD. Again there is debate on the Date. But they do agree it was a number of years after the death, burial and resurrection of Jesus and his ascension to the right hand of the Father. (Acts 1:9-11)

So What does this mean for us?

When Jesus makes a statement, especially one like: "*have the faith of God, Let the faith of God be in you,*" We can rest assured that is a true statement and it is available.

But was he speaking to the disciples only or was he speaking this truth to future generations of believers and disciples?

The disciples at that time were not able to be spiritually renewed, they were still under the Old Covenant Law and living by the rules. They had a great three year transition into the New Covenant. Where Jesus fulfilled the Law of Moses and opened the door to God's grace, in which we have direct communication with God. This was done by his death on the cross, his burial and resurrection.

After this great event, right standing with God had become available for anyone who would believe in the name of Jesus and truly submit themselves to him.

A new spirit became available to the believer, one that is the same as God, Jesus and the Holy Spirit. It is sealed with the stamp of the Holy Spirit, the seal is as one would place a seal on an important document. I heard one preacher say that our spirit is sealed by the Holy Spirit as you would vacuum pack food.

It is freed from the contamination of the outside world. The new spirit in you is fully grown and developed, it is not a baby spirit.

Faith was available to people prior to Jesus's death and resurrection, we can see this in number of scriptures throughout the Old Testament and in the gospels.

Starting in the gospels we see evidence in Mark 5: 21-25 and 35 – 42 The story of Jairus and his daughter. Jairus was a ruler of the synagogue, he was a man of some statue and credence within the community, Rulers of a synagogue were the third highest ranking official. We see in verse 23 "*and he begged him earnestly' my little daughter lies at the point of death. Come and lay your hands on her that she may be healed and she will live'*"NKJV

Mark 5: 25-34 The woman with the issue of blood, this lady was in all sorts of discomfort and was in dire need of healing. It took a lot of intestinal fortitude for her to be out in public, according to Leviticus 15: 25-27 she was classed as unclean due to her condition. According to the law everything she touches becomes unclean or anything that touches her will become unclean. But despite this when she heard about Jesus she knew she had a hope of being made well.

The Bible tells us she heard about Jesus, she believed that if she touched his garment his would be made well, *"for she said if only I may touch his clothes. I shall be made well"* vs 28 NKJV

The outcome was she got what her faith demanded of the power of God in Jesus.

And Jesus said to her, "*Daughter your faith has made you well, Go in Peace and be healed of your affliction" vs 34.*NKJV

The Centurion in Matthew 8: 5-13 is another great example of the use of faith. A centurion was a professional officer in the Roman army, and in charge of 100 soldiers, a centura. These guys were true leaders, they lead from the front, they understood leadership and authority. They were normally promoted from the ranks, so they were not novices. They displayed courage and leadership. They were in charge of discipline of the troops, and other duties. It is now easier to see that the centurion in question understood authority, he recognised who Jesus was and the authority he carried.

In verse 6 the centurion spoke to Jesus and explained the situation and Jesus was very willing to go to his house but this great statement of faith that came out of the mouth of the centurion made Jesus marvel.

Verse 8 "*The centurion answered and said I am not worthy that you should come under my roof but only speak a word and my servant will be healed*" NKJV This ended in a very positive result, the servant was healed.

These are only three of the more popular instances of the use of faith prior to Jesus' death and resurrection. If you search out the Old Testament you will find a number of occasions where people had faith in God. The place to start is to look at the 'Hall of Fame' of faith champions in the book of Hebrews. There is much to be said about these scriptures but that is for another time. The point is that faith was available. It was used to accomplish great things.

In the three scriptures mentioned above, all three had things in common in their stories. Remember these were real stories, real people with real needs. Jesus met every need through faith in him.

This faith drew the power out of him, we confirm this in the example of the woman who had the issue of blood. Mark 5: 30

says "*and Jesus, immediately knowing that power had gone out of him, turned around in the crowd and said 'Who touched my clothes?'*"

Verse 34 "*Daughter, your faith has made you well, Go in peace and be healed of your affliction*" NKJV

Oh what power has faith to connect to the great and mighty anointing of God.

What are the things these people had in common that got the results they needed?

1. They had a need;
2. They knew Jesus was the answer, they knew his authority;
3. They humbled themselves and took risks;
4. They all spoke what they needed;
5. They did not listen or take notice of the negative;
6. They all received.

The pattern is very similar to the father of faith, Abraham (Rom. 4). All of the Old testament believers gained the things from God by faith. So faith was available to them.

Here we are today as Born again spirit filled believers, who have completely reborn spirits full of the character and power of God, and we cannot believe for $10. Don't be offended but I have witnessed first hand these things, not just in my life.

I remember in a church I was attending there was a lady who was supposed to be a pillar of the church, always having a word for someone and wanting to move in the gifts of the Spirit. More accurately wanted the spectacular. She attended church every week. This lady had a business, was self employed, but come Monday morning when her business was open and no customers and no sales, she panicked and rang her Pastor to pray for her business.

Where was her faith? Especially after the message on Sunday was on Faith and your right standing with God. Her faith was not in God's promises but in her Pastor. I am not against praying for others especially the prayer of agreement, but our faith should be in the promises of God. I also believe that the Pastor had a case to answer because he was enabling her to continue in unbelief and thus preventing her from establishing victory in her life.

It was a great lesson for me to stand on God's promises and find the victory through Faith in God's word rather than faith in a man. To get prayer from others is a good thing but to run to them in panic means you have you have not even attempted to use the faith in you. I believe that you take God's word meditate on it, see it, confess it, act on it and then go to the pastor and get into agreement with him/her and the word.

Folks don't put your entire trust in people, they will at some point disappoint you and unwittingly offend you. Our Trust has always been in God's word, as it does not lie, allow the great things in side you, coming from your spirit to lead you. (Gal.5: 22-23)

Back to the original question:

So What does this mean for us and was he speaking to the disciples only or was he speaking this truth to future generations of believers and disciples?

It is my belief that Jesus was talking to both disciples at that time and future generations of disciples and or believers. His teaching was on how the Faith of God works and as per the examples used here, when the principles of faith are put to use every mountain in the lives of those who used it were removed and cast in to the sea, gone forever.

If we notice in the three examples of faith, in the above scriptures, each time they called upon Jesus to manifest the healing. Each case it was their faith that drew out the healing virtue.

In the days after the death burial and resurrection of Jesus, when Jesus open the door to the Father and the door of being born again, gaining the full access to all of heavens benefits. We no longer have call on Jesus to heal us. Because it is done, we already have it. In two places the Bible states "by his wounds he has healed us". Once in Isaiah, where he is looking toward the future to the cross and another in 1 Peter 2:24 where he is looking back in hind sight to the cross.

Isaiah 53: 4-5 says, *"Surely He has born our griefs and carried our sorrows; Yet we esteemed him stricken, Smitten of God and afflicted. But he was wounded for our Transgressions, He was bruised for our iniquities: The chastisement for our peace was upon him and by his stripes we are healed"* NKJV

1 Peter 2: 24 says, *"Who Himself bore our sins in His own body on the tree, that we having died to sins, might live unto righteousness- by whose strips we are healed."* NKJV

Paul confirms these in Romans 10: 6-9 *"But the righteousness of faith speaks in this way, "Do not say in your heart, 'Who will ascend into heaven?'"* (that is, to bring Christ down from above) *or, "'Who will descend into the abyss?'"* (that is, to bring Christ up from the dead). *But what does it say? "The word is near you, in your mouth and in your heart" (that is, the word of faith which we preach): that if you confess with your mouth the Lord Jesus and believe in your heart that God has raised Him from the dead, you will be saved.* NKJV

We can see that healing is already prepared for us in the new Covenant and it is accessed by the Word in your mouth and the Word in your heart. Your healing has been established, it is yours. Jesus got it for you when he took the stripes.

In the gospel accounts that we read the faith of people drew the healing power out of Jesus.

However for us today that healing power is inside of us, it is not our power but the power of God that Jesus won for us at the cross.

Instead of drawing the power out of Jesus, our faith draws on the power that is within us, it is definitely Gods power not ours, (Eph. 3:20)

Peter and John, disciples of Jesus, understood this. In Acts 3: 1-16 at the Gate Beautiful there was a man lame from birth, notice Peter and John did not say ' come Lord Jesus and heal this man', No that is total unbelief. They were operating in the power of the Holy Spirit and under the Authority of the Word of God, Mark 16: 15-18. We see in verse 17-18 it says, "***And these signs will follow those who believe: in my name they will*** *cast out demons, they will speak with new tongues; They will take up serpents, drink any thing deadly, it will by no means hurt them;* ***they will lay hands on the sick and they shall recover."*** NKJV

They believed in the Word of God, they had faith in the name of Jesus and the words of Jesus came to pass and was a reality.

Faith is in your heart and the release of this powerful force is by your mouth.

Every believer has this faith inside them, meditate the Word, see it on the inside of you, use that imagination, say it and use it.

Chapter THREE

WHERE IS FAITH?

We know from reading the Bible that God is the originator of all things, there is no counterfeit in God. He is the creator of All. Genesis chapter 1 tells us the story of God's creation and his great creative power. He saw what he wanted and weighed and measured it (Is. 40: 12). He spoke it, the Word of God (Jesus), the Holy Spirit took those words and incubated them.(Gen. 1: 2) Like a mother hen sits on eggs, making sure they came into being. The rest is history.

This creative power came about because God always speaks life, he always believes what he says and it is always right.

This same faith that created everything, was given to believers in Christ at the very moment of the spiritual new birth. Romans 12: 3 KJV says "….*but to think soberly, accordingly as God hath dealt to every man the measure of faith.*" To think soberly meaning: not to think more highly or lowly of yourself, than others because you are all equal and it is the exact same measure given to every one. We know the Author is writing to believers because of the context of the chapter.

The originator of your faith is God, he imparts his faith to you. It is the perfect measure. But it is what we do with that measure that causes great things to happen in your life.

This faith is God's own personal faith, he freely gives it to anyone who chooses Christ.

God's very own faith resides on the inside of you, ready to create and bring into manifestation all of the benefits and promises of God. It is by his mighty Grace that he chooses to impart this great gift to anyone who is willing to receive Christ as Lord and Saviour. It is available to all (John 3: 16; Rom. 2: 11; 2 Cor. 5:15-21; 1John 2: 2).

Mark 11: 22 makes a bit more sense now, "*Have the God kind of faith*" because its already in you.

If we realise what a great gift we have inside us, if we stop our busy lives for a moment and think, ponder and meditate on such a wonder gift that has been imparted to us. God himself in us, nothing is impossible, fear becomes obsolete, the cares of the world don't "*enter in*"(Mark 4: 19). The cares of the world are always present but don't let them enter in and rob you. We become good ground ready to produce much fruit, unlike the fruitless fig tree.

This is not the first time God put himself into man. In Genesis when God created man, he created him in his own image and likeness.

Genesis 1: 26 says, "*Then God said 'Let us make man in our image, according to our likeness.*" NKJV

Man was to be the exact replica of God. Inside and out.

Genesis 1: 27 says, "*So God created man in his own image, in the image of God he created him, male and female.*" NKJV

I was reading this one day and the Spirit of God said to me, "have you noticed that image is mentioned twice in this scripture, do you know why?"

Of course being as quick as I am, I responded, "No".

He said "because God's creative power is in his imagination, exactly like yours." That is when I realised that God saw man in his imagination, this where hope comes from, as an image before he created him.

We are the same.

The Formation of Man

Genesis 2: 7 says, *"And the Lord formed man of the dust of the ground and breathed life into his nostrils, the breath of life; and man became a living being."* NKJV

This was very personal to God, he personally took the time to create man, he created from the dust of the ground, with the exact dimensions and detail that he saw in his imagination. He formed, moulded us with his very own hands. What a great honour for us to be personally detailed by the great creator.

But that's not the end of it, He then proceeded to breath life into man with his very own breath. This breath contains life, the very life of God himself. God breathed himself into man. Inside man contained everything God is and has. We owe everything to God.

That life which God breathed into man connected Man with God. Adam had the mind of God, He thought like God, His nature was that like God. He was intelligent like God. This had to be the case because he was created in the very likeness of God. (Gen. 1:26). Adam named every living creature (Gen. 2: 19-20). That shows an intelligent being.

But unfortunately God's man, Adam, made a very bad decision. This decision cost him and the rest of humanity to loose the Life that God has input into man at his creation.

So man lost the Life of God and this caused the separation of God and man. Man's Life Nature, God's Nature, with its vitality was replaced with the nature of a selfish, self centred, ugly fallen angel, full of iniquity and in opposition to everything about God. This nature has none of the God life in it.

After this act of treason, man became ashamed and became fearful of God (Gen. 3: 7-10). This is a first for Adam and Eve, they were never ashamed before and was never fearful before (Gen. 2:25). We can see the change in nature and therefore in thought.

But thanks be unto God the great and merciful one, He initiated his plan to the breathe his life, with it's God nature back into man, though faith in His Son Jesus the Anointed.

So now we know that Gods very own personal faith is inside every born again believer. As discussed previously this happens at the very moment of our acceptance of Jesus Christ, it is in equal amount given to all who believe.

It is the same faith that created the universe, the same faith that Jesus used in every miracle and healing. It is in you. It is a spiritual force ready and waiting to be used by you to bring about God's promises to the world.

God is so clever and way smarter than any man, the Bible says, "*faith comes by hearing and hearing by the Word of God.*" Rom. 10: 17. When people hear the word of God and that seed of the word enters in to them and they accept it, it is faith that causes them to accept it. This is the faith that God gives us, it is his faith to be born again.

So faith is in us, God's faith, so when put to work it accomplishes where it is sent.

This great spiritual force is your servant and wants to be put to work. It is like a kelpie dog just always ready to be put to work, ready to bring in the sheep and or cattle as the dogs owner decides. So is the faith you have inside always ready to be used to bring in the promises of God.

But faith has some helpers along side it. Hope and Love. (1Cor.13:13)

Chapter FOUR

FAITH AND HOPE

Faith and Hope work very closely together, some people at times find it difficult to know the difference. I have heard the faith purest say, don't hope just use your faith.

Those people who are successful in their faith walk are using Hope without recognising it. So understanding and using Hope will sky rocket your faith.

Hope is what you see inside yourself, the images you see. But more on that later.

Faith is what you do with what you see. The action taken.

Hebrews 11: 1 says, "*Now faith is the substance of things hoped for, the evidence of things not seen.*" NKJV

The Passion Translation says it this way "*Now faith brings our hopes into reality and the foundation needed to acquire the things we long for. It is the evidence required to prove what is still unseen.*" The only place anything is unseen is in the natural, things you cannot see with the natural eye. The things that are unseen are really seen in your imagination and not with the natural eye.

It is with the imagination that you develop the inner image, called Hope. Hence the name Imag- in – ation, it almost looks like Image in Action.

Perhaps that's a better name for Faith. Image in Action.

There is a scripture that talks about the Loins of your mind, 1Peter 1: 13 says, "*Therefore gird up the loins of your mind, be sober, and rest your Hope fully on the grace that is to be brought to you at the revelation of Jesus Christ.*"

What is meant by the 'loins of your mind', the loins of a human body is the reproductive parts, the place of fertility. This where the human body reproduces.

The loins of the mind works in a similar fashion, it is the fertile, reproductive parts of the mind. This part is commonly called the imagination. It is where you reproduce what ever you think about. What ever you think upon, ponder, consider, meditate on, these are things that will be produced in your life. Paul understood this in Philippians 4:8, "*Finally brethren, whatever things are true, whatever things are noble, whatever things are just, whatever things are pure, whatever things are lovely, whatever things are lovely, whatever things are of good report, if there is any virtue and if there is anything praiseworthy- meditate on these things*" NKJV

If we do this, it will change our lives and positive things will be produced, needless to say you find the absence of anxiety also.

Have you heard the term: "looking at things through the eye of faith", have you ever wondered what that really means? I would suggest the eye of faith is what the New Testament calls Hope, it is what you see through your imagination, you see the destination, the direction to the end result first in your inner self. Then Faith is the walking out of what you see. It gives you a reference point, to always come back to when needed. Hope anchors your soul, it causes you to be steadfast.

Hebrews 6: 19 says, "*This Hope we have as an anchor of the soul, sure and steadfast....*"

Hope is the anchor that stops us from swaying to and fro, causes us to be sure and established.

From the Vine's expository Dictionary of the New Testament we see the definition of Hope in the NT, *"favourable and confident expectation"*. It has to do with the unseen and the future, "Hope" describes a happy anticipation of Good.

To give a practical application of Hope or confident expectation, we compare Hope to a set of building plans, some countries call them Blue Prints. These plans show us what to expect when the building is built, what the building is going to look like and how it is to be built. They also give not just the owner but the builder what to expect when building is being built and the end result. Both the builder and the owner have an expectation on how the building will turn out. The building should be exactly what is on the plans. These plans start with a desire or an idea that is put down on paper.

Faith is the action to Hope therefore in the case of the building, faith/action is actually building the building. The end result is you get what you saw within your self. God did this in Genesis, hence this is why God said a few times "*it is good*" because the end result was exactly what he had seen in his imagination. Exactly as he had planned.

Another example is that of a packet of seeds. When you go to the garden shop or wherever they sell seeds in your country, the packet of seeds has a picture on the front and the instructions on the back, with the seeds inside the packet. The picture on the front is our expectation (Hope) of what we get when we plant the seed. The instructions on the back is how to use the seed (Word of God), Faith is when we follow the instructions and put action to our hope (expectation) by planting the seeds. After the allotted time (patient endurance) we should get exactly what the image on the front of the packet of seeds. Therefore Hope (inner image, expectation) is fulfilled by action or doing (Faith). If you don't act then you cannot expect a result.

Think like God, Act like God

This is the same pattern of Hope and Faith that God uses. The book of Genesis shows us this. If we pattern our selves in the same fashion as God, we will get the same results that God gets. When we start having the same success as God does then our Heart will not grow sick because our Hope is not deferred.

Isaiah 55: 8 says, "*For My thoughts are not your thoughts, Nor are your ways My ways, says the Lord. For as the heavens are higher than the earth, so are my ways higher than your ways, And my thoughts higher than your thoughts.*" NKJV

Not once does God say you cannot have his thoughts or operate in his ways, he is pointing out that his ways are far superior to ours and his thoughts are far superior than ours. He wants us to think like him and operate like him, otherwise he would not have said "*......But we have the mind of Christ.*" 1Cor. 2: 16 and 1 Cor. 2: 10-13 "*But God has revealed them to us through His Spirit. For the Spirit searches all things, yes, the deep things of God. For what man knows the things of a man except the spirit of the man which is in him? Even so no one knows the things of God except the Spirit of God. Now we have received, not the spirit of the world, but the Spirit who is from God, that we might know the things that have been freely given to us by God. These things we also speak, not in words which man's wisdom teaches but which the Holy Spirit teaches, comparing spiritual things with spiritual.*" NKJV

God shows us his ways and thoughts through his Word and his Spirit.

God's way of doing things

God's way of doing things is always right. His purpose is always pure and always to benefit us. His method is faith motivated by Love, as that is who he is (1 John 4: 8).

If we look at the way God does things, we see in Genesis 1:1 God created, Verse 3 onwards "God said ". We see that the release of God's word is mighty powerful, then the Holy Spirit took those words and made them come to pass. The Father, the Word and the Holy Spirit worked perfectly together to create.

My question is: How did God know what to say? God is not random, he does not just all of a sudden change his mind, He is not double minded, His thoughts are not all over the place.

He just doesn't randomly say stuff. He is intelligent, He is thoughtful, He knows exactly what he is doing at all times. So how did He know what to say?

I believe One answer is in found in Isaiah 40: 12 "*Who has measured the waters in the hollow of his hand, Measured heaven with a span and calculated the dust of the earth in a measure? Weighed the mountains in scales and the Hills in a balance.*" NKJV

God has already seen it before he spoke it, before his faith filled words created it. Another place is in Genesis again we look at Verse 26 "*God said let us make man in our image according to our likeness.....*" God already saw what man looked like before he formed him and Breathed his life into man. God used his imagination to create, then he released it by his words and acted on the inner image, to create. This is what we call Hope and then faith that gives substance to hope. Faith causes the unseen to become seen.

It is God's word that gives us Hope and Faith. What I'm saying is what God saw in Himself is what he expected to happen and it did. We are the same as we are made in his likeness.

Many Examples to Follow

If we look into the heroes of faith in Hebrews chapter 11 from verses 7 - 13 we see that they did great things through faith but in verse 13 it says "*These all died in faith, not having received the promises but having seen them from afar off were assured of them, embraced them and confessed that they were strangers and pilgrims on earth.*" NKJV

These people saw the promises, albeit from a distance but they still saw them. How could they see something that was not yet manifested, unless they only considered the promises and saw the them as an image on the inside, that image anchored their soul and gave their faith something to work with.

Joshua son of Nun

Another example to look is Joshua, what a good man he was, Moses right hand man. Joshua was a man who cut through the garbage of unbelief of the 10 spies, these are the 10 who went weak at the knees. Joshua gave a good report and knew if they acted on what God had said they would gain the promise. (Numbers 13 and 14: 1-9).

If we skip forward 40 odd years, Moses has died and the Israelite folks were still in the wilderness and God spoke to Joshua the son of Nun.

Joshua was instructed to keep the Law, for us these days it's converted into the Word of God, in his mouth, continually confess it and to meditate on it, this keeps it in his heart. In other words he was only to consider the Law (Word of God) and not to consider anything else.

Keeping it in his mouth and in his heart, it built a strong image of victory inside him, He realised that following God's instruction he would not loose but have victory.

In verse 8 of the Book of Joshua it says "*The Book of the Law (Word) shall not depart from your mouth, but you shall meditate in it day and night, that you may observe to do according to all that is written in it. For then you will make your way prosperous and then you will have good success.*" NKJV

Notice he was to continually talk success, he was to meditate on the word this caused him to see success as an image (Hope). Then he was to see to it that 'he did' or 'acted upon' what the word said (Faith) and the end result is prosperity and good success. What made him act on the word and have success? He saw the image of success in himself. He knew God cannot lie, God is full to overflowing with integrity, He knew if he followed God's instructions he would get the result that was promised.

I don't know about you but I much prefer to carry around, inside me, the image of victory than defeat.

Hope says "I see it", Faith says "oh good, I'll go get it."

Chapter FIVE

LAW OF FAITH

Firstly lets clarify the word Law, don't be confused between the Law of Faith and the Law of Moses. The Law of Moses was given to a lawless people, who wanted to be a law unto themselves. The Law of Moses was designed to show humanity that they cannot save themselves but are in desperate need of a Savior.

The law of Faith is a spiritual law that works for whoever chooses to use it. Similarly we see natural laws, for example, the more common and easy to understand law, the Law of Gravity.

What goes up must come down. Sir Isaac Newton who discovered the Physical laws of Gravity and Motion opened up an amazing doorway for mankind.

The Physical law of gravity can be over ridden by higher physical laws such as The Law of Lift, Drag and Thrust or the Law of lighter than air. We see these physical laws working everyday in aircraft, gliders and hot air balloons. But it does seem as though the Law of Gravity gets its way and everything eventually lands.

A Law is something that works for anyone, anywhere at anytime. These Physical Laws have been around since the beginning of what know as time. They would have worked in the time of Jesus if these laws were know. I heard one man say "do you think 747 aircraft could have flown in the time of Jesus? Well of course the answer is Yes, had the laws of Lift, Drag and Thrust been know and developed. Not to mention the materials and knowledge to build and fly it. But the point is the physical laws will always work for anyone who makes a decision to use them.

So is Spiritual laws, they have been around longer than physical laws, We can see God using the Law of Faith at creation, (Gen.1) before we had an atmosphere and gravity on earth. Spiritual Laws have always been and will work for anyone, whoever, decides to use them. They work anytime, anywhere and for anyone.

Again Jesus is demonstrating the Law of Faith in the story of the Fig Tree.

Mark 11:23 says, *"For assuredly, I say to you, whoever says to this mountain, 'Be removed and be cast into the sea,' and does not doubt in his heart, but believes that those things he says will be done, he will have whatever he says."* NKJV

The scripture in Mark 11:22-26 is a great tutorial on How God's faith works. That faith is inside every believer.

This passage of scripture starts off by Jesus saying in verse 23, "*For assuredly, I say to you…*"

The word *assuredly*, means: *truthfully, without a doubt, unquestionably, with absolute certainty.*

We know that Jesus cannot lie, so if he says *"assuredly, truly, verily"* then he is emphasising the absolute truth in the matter. We need not look further except to believe what he says.

"For assuredly, I say to you, whoever says to this mountain, 'Be removed and be cast into the sea,' and does not doubt in his heart......"

Jesus performed this exactly when calming the storm in Mark 4 35-41. Faith filled words, getting the same result as the fig tree and getting the same reaction from his disciples.

In Mark 4: 35 – 41 Jesus and his disciples were in a boat and Jesus was asleep in the stern. A great wind storm came, and great means great. In this case a great wind storm isn't just a gusty day which cases a bit of a rough sea, this was so great a wind storm that it stirred the waters to the point of swamping the boat. It must have been terrifying.

They woke up Jesus and he rebuked the storm, saying *"peace, be still."*(v 38) and there was a great calm (v 38). Again great means great, the calm must have been perfect calm, the exact opposite to the storm. The disciples feared and said who is this guy, the winds, the sea obey him. I find it interesting that, like the fig tree, the weather and the sea was being rebellious. The elements were opposing the words of Jesus in verse 35 where Jesus said, "*Let us cross over to the other side."*

Jesus using the same principles as he did in the story if the fig tree. Used his faith and authority to stop the storm, He released his faith and authority by speaking to the storm. He did not speak just any words, he spoke exactly what he wanted.

Whoever

"Whoever" Jesus points out that this is available and will work for anyone, at any time and at anywhere. The only qualification you need to use this Spiritual Law, is to be alive and breathing. Whoever means ***whoever***.

Whosoever says

When Jesus says, "whoever says," He shows that faith is released through the mouth, expressed in words. Our words carry power—they create and set things in motion. Spoken in faith, they release a spiritual force that brings what is believed into reality.

Whether positive or negative, our words carry power. In James 3:1–12, the tongue is compared to a ship's rudder—small, yet able to determine direction. What we say matters deeply.

So what gives the tongue such influence? It is simply another way of describing our words—the things we speak each day.

The Bible tells us in Luke 6:45, *"A good man out of the good treasure in his heart brings forth good; and an evil man out of the evil treasure in his heart brings forth evil.* ***For out of the abundance of the heart the mouth speaks."*** NKJV

So how do things come to fill the heart in abundance? Once again, we must turn to the Bible for the answer.

Proverbs 23: 7 says, "……***As a man thinks in his heart, so is he****……."*

What you think upon, what you consider, meditate on, what you ponder on, what you listen to, what you watch, what you allow into your thoughts and let them stay there, they will form a picture inside you. These inner images find there way into your heart, formulate ideas, and congregate in abundance in your heart. This is what comes out of your mouth when the pressure is on.

If I don't like what I say can I change it? Yes 100%, change what you watch, what you confess, what you think about and start meditating on the truth, God's word is truth.

Plant the seed of God's word into your heart and we can see such great positive results, such as we see in Mark 4: 30-32 NKJV, *"Then He said 'To what shall we liken the Kingdom of God?*

Or with what parable shall we picture it? It is like a grain of mustard seed which when sown on the ground, is smaller than all the seeds on the earth; but when it is sown, it grows up and becomes greater than all herbs, and shoots out large branches, so that the birds of the air may nest under its shade." Oh this is a great picture of what the Word of God does when planted in the ground, the heart of a person. It becomes greater than anything in the garden of your heart. Even the birds of the air rest there, these birds were previously stealing the seed of the word (Mark 4: 4) but now have no power and come to nothing. Plant the word, read it, meditate on it, consider it, ponder on it and watch the garden of your heart grow great things.

The Mountain

"Whoever says to this mountain, 'Be removed and be cast into the sea,'"

Oh dear no, the dreaded mountain. I know the cynics will say 'impossible', well it is for them. But I much prefer to take Jesus' word for it than their word.

Jesus cannot lie.

To show us how powerful the Law of Faith is, Jesus used the mountains that were in view at the time to teach us. To the natural mind this is an impossibility, with out the use of machinery and explosives. In that era there were no earth moving equipment or explosives as we know them today. Maybe they had the manually operated front end loader, we know as a shovel or the manually operated excavator, we know as a garden hoe or a pick mattock.

Regardless, to the natural mind it seems as impossible then as it does now.

This indicates to me that Jesus emphasised how powerful the Law of Faith really is. I also believe that by using the mountain as an example it formulated a picture inside the disciples on the power of faith.

Just for a moment, humour me and without any preconceived ideas or cynical thoughts, using your imagination see yourself speaking your faith filled words to a mountain. See it disappear before your eyes.

Hopefully you can see that mountain being moved. Hopefully it creates an image, in you, of the power of the Law of Faith. That nothing is impossible for you who believe. (Mark 9: 23) All things are possible.

Most of us live very normal everyday lives. We are not about to bust a move and flatten ever physical mountain we see. These physical mountains are a thing of beauty, snow capped mountains of New Zealand or Japan and the ruggedness of the Australian or South African mountain ranges. All of these show us the creative genius of God. As I said before, Jesus is illustrating the power that is in words of faith. This is how we access what in the natural is impossible. So what relevance is the mountain to us? In the case of most of us the mountain is symbolic of problems we face. It can also be a situation that stands in the way of achieving a desired goal.

Remember Mark11: 23-24 is talking about speaking directly to the mountain, it is not about confessing God's promises. Although confession of God's word is very important, it is not the theme of Jesus' teaching here.

I was listening to a preacher talk of a Lady that came to his services for prayer for healing. She was battling chronic pain, this pain was extremely debilitating and caused her great distress. In a great piece of ministering, He explained to her not to pray to God about the pain but to speak directly to the chronic pain (Rom. 10: 6-9). This preacher acted on what he believed and spoke directly to the pain, in the Name of Jesus he told it to go and it did.

He understood and used the law of faith. But the lady said I have this different pain and is still there. The preacher said now you work it" She prayed a pray of thanksgiving and confessed her healing, she did not blame God for the pain but it did not go. Simply because she didn't pray the way Jesus taught us to pray.

As soon as she realised that it was ineffectual, she spoke to the pain in the name of Jesus and it left her.

The lesson to learn here is to confess God's word is exactly correct and has great benefit for your life, but The Law of Faith says to speak directly to the mountain. Whatever it is saying to you, answer it direct.

Things speak to you

In the case of the fig tree in Mark 11: 13-14, *"And seeing from afar a fig tree having leaves, He went to if perhaps to see if he would find something on it. When he came to it, He found nothing but leaves, for it was not the season for figs."14 "In response Jesus said to it, Let no one eat from you ever again."* NKJV

Did you notice Jesus responded to the fig tree? So the fig tree was saying something to Jesus, perhaps it said, 'No figs today, I might look like a fig tree with my pretty leaves but I have nothing for you, bad luck mate'.

So we see the fig tree gave non verbal communication, if it wasn't communicating to Jesus then the Bible would not have said, *"In response, Jesus said...."* so we see that Jesus answered the fig tree and spoke directly to it.

Remember the account of the storm in Mark 4:35–41. Jesus had already declared, *"Let us go to the other side."* Yet the storm seemed to rise in defiance of that word, as if it had a voice of its own saying, *"Not today—you will not cross."*

But Jesus responded. He rebuked the storm, silenced its threat, and replaced chaos with peace. In effect, His answer was, *"Yes, we are going to the other side. Nothing will prevent My word from being fulfilled. Peace, be still."*

Some might say, "Oh but he was Jesus the Anointed, He is the Son of God with power and authority." All of that is true. He also gave us the same power and authority to continue his works on this earth. It is still him who does the work through us. Here are a few scriptures that show us our authority on this earth through Jesus;

Mark 16; 15-18 ; John 14: 12 ; Ephesians 2; 19 ; Luke 10 :19

Just as the fig tree and the storm spoke to Jesus so we have things in our everyday life that speak to us, our bills speak to us. They are hanging around on the fridge door, having a good time until you walk past and they call out to you, "Hey, I have to be paid and you don't have the money."

Bank accounts are the same and so on and so forth.

Your health is another thing that speaks to you, every time you have an ache or pain it's talking. The doctors reports also have a voice.

So what do we do? These things can be frightening and debilitating, they cause anxiety, depression, fear. If dwelt upon they strip you of your faith.

We read in Proverbs 12: 25, "*Anxiety in the heart of man causes depression.*"

Take the example of Jesus and respond to your bills, to your bank account, to the doctors report or that aching joint. Speak to them with faith filled words and destroy their ability to cripple you. Answer straight. Speak the truth to the storms of life, to the mountains.

Faith is action and released through words. Take God's word and destroy your enemy.

The examples of Jesus are how he believed what he said, these examples are all through the four Gospels.

We have the excellent example of the law of faith in the fig tree story but another that comes to mind is when Jesus raised Lazarus from the dead.

John 11: 1-44 is the story of a friend of Jesus, a man by the name of Lazarus. There is much to learn in this story but the area for this writing is from verse 40-44. So Lazarus had died and was buried in a tomb, The relatives of Lazarus put the blame onto Jesus, as people do these days because people don't take the time to understand God or his ways.

Jesus instructed them to remove the stone that was covering the opening to the tomb. In verse 43 we see Jesus operating the Law of Faith perfectly and got the result that he wanted.

"Now when He had said these things, he cried with a loud voice" Lazarus come forth!" (44) "And he who had died came out bound hand and foot with grave clothes and his face was wrapped with a cloth. Jesus said "Loose him and let him go" NKJV

Do we realise this same power that proceeds from God is totally available to us,

This is Jesus' own words. Peter and the rest of the disciples understood this.

Disciples used what they learnt

Acts 3:1-8 NKJV says,

"Now Peter and John went up together to the temple at the hour of prayer,the ninth hour. And a certain man lame from his mother's womb was carried, whom they laid daily at the gate of the temple which is called Beautiful,to ask alms from those who entered the temple;who, seeing Peter and John about to go into the temple, asked

for alms. And fixing his eyes on him, with John, Peter said, "Look at us." So he gave them his attention, expecting to receive something from them. Then Peter said, "Silver and gold I do not have, but what I do have I give you. In the name of Jesus Christ of Nazareth, rise up and walk."And he took him by the right hand and lifted him up, and immediately his feet and ankle bones received strength. So he, leaping up, stood and walked and entered the *temple with them—walking, leaping, and praising God."*

Peter and John were going to the temple to pray. As they came to the temple they saw this lame man, he was in the strategic position, he was at the gate. This gate was the entrance to the temple. This man was lame from birth and sat at this gate every day to beg for money. When he got the attention of Peter and John, little did he realise his life was about to dramatically change. Peter and John understood the power in the name of Jesus and because the lesson of the fig tree, they understood the power and how to release the law of faith. They knew inside themselves they have been given the authority to use the name of Jesus. The other thing they knew was they had the Holy Spirit with them, whose power and wisdom is unmatched. Also they knew how to release the Law of faith, they knew it is released by speaking to the lame mans mountain.

Did you also notice they did not pray to God or Jesus to come and heal the man, they understood that the mans' healing and being made whole had been accomplished by the stripes that Jesus suffered. (1Peter 2: 24) It needed to be activated through faith. The power of God is released through believing in your heart and released through your words.

Mark 16: 17-18 NKJV, "*And these signs will follow those who believe. In My name they will cast out demons; they will speak with new tongues. They will take up serpents and if they drink any thing deadly it will by no means hurt them; they will lay hands on the sick and they will recover.*"

They took that word, that Jesus personally spoke to them, and made it their own. They knew that Jesus cannot lie therefore that word was theirs and in them. They acted on it.

Notice it says: "*And these signs will follow those who believe: In My name they will ……*"

I like to look at this part of this scripture and say "*these sign will follow those who believe in my name and in my Name they will…..*" Not only has the name of Jesus have such great authority but as we do things in his name, we are his representatives. Just as an ambassador represents his or her country. They have the total backing of that country and the authority that accompanies it. So do we have the total backing in authority and power of the Kingdom of God. Notice the Peter and John spoke directly to the problem they didn't confess scripture nor did they pray to God to come down and heal him. They understood how Faith worked they understood their authority.

Just as a side note if we look in verse 10 of Acts 3 "T*hen they knew that it was he who sat begging alms at the Beautiful gate of the Temple and they were* ***filled with wonder and amazement*** *at what had happened to him."* NKJV

Take note they were filled with wonder and amazement and not filled with faith. It would seem that miracles get the attention of people and give them Hope, miracles can point people in the direction of the Word but it is hearing the Word of God that they gain faith.

Because we know that faith comes by hearing and hearing by the word of God (Rom. 10: 17).

This is my thoughts on this matter as I read that scripture.

No Doubt in your heart. How to keep doubt out.

As we work our way through Mark 11: 22-26 we come to the section on '*no doubt*' but '*Believe in those things that he says it will happen*'.

"So Jesus answered and said to them, "Have faith in God. For assuredly, I say to you, whoever says to this mountain, 'Be removed and be cast into the sea,' ***and does not doubt in his heart, but believes that those things he says will be done, he will have whatever he says.***

Having no doubt in your heart and believe what you say are closely related. Doubt in your heart is different from having a doubtful thought. Kenneth E Hagin, who ministered a lot on Mark 11: 22-26, said this about thoughts, you can't stop a bird from flying over your head but you can certainly can stop it from landing. This is my take on what he said and it is so true. If you have a doubtful thought dismiss it immediately, think on what you see inside yourself, think on the promise, think on the end result of what you believe you receive. This is what stops the thought from landing and finding it's way into your heart. Say 'NO' to that doubting thought.

Where doubt comes into the heart is when you consider and think on, ponder on the negative thought. This is when it becomes a problem, we must learn to control our thoughts. Speak and meditate on God's word.

Another hint on getting rid of doubt in the heart is found in Philemon verse 6: *"That the sharing of your* ***faith may become effectual*** *by the acknowledgement of every good thing which is in you in Christ Jesus."*

Know who you are, Know what he has done for you, Know what God has deposited inside you. Know you have right standing with God, Know you have the Holy Spirit inside you, Know you have the nature and character of God, Know that you have access to all of the kingdom of God. We say we know but we don't really marinate in it long enough to get the fullness of understanding. If we start to allow these truths to settle inside of us, boldness and Faith arise. Be diligent and determined.

Nothing will be impossible. Your Faith will become very effective.

Fear produces doubt, if we take the example of Jesus and the disciples as they cross the sea of Galilee. Matthew 8: 23-27 " *Now when He got into a boat, His disciples followed Him. And suddenly a great tempest arose on the sea, so that the boat was covered with the waves. But He was asleep. Then His disciples came to Him and awoke Him, saying, "Lord, save us! We are perishing!" But He said to them,* ***"Why are you fearful, O you of little faith?"*** *Then He arose and* ***rebuked the winds and the sea, and there was a great calm.*** *So the men marvelled, saying, "Who can this be, that even the winds and the sea obey Him?"* NKJV

Fear stole every ounce of hope and faith that the disciples had, also notice the method Jesus used to rebuke the storm.....The Law of Faith... he spoke to it.

Abraham

I would like to share with you the story of Abraham and how he stopped doubt from 'entering in'.

Abraham's story starts in Genesis 12 to Chapter 25. It tells us about his life from the time God spoke to him at the age of 75 up until his death at 175 years old.

Originally He was called Abram, meaning exalted father. According to Dr. Eli Lizorkin-Eyzenberg and Rev. Jim Stowe The name "Abram" *(Avram)* is composed of two words, av and ram, and means something like "exalted father."

Abraham *(Avraham),* on the other hand, derives from the words *av)* and *(hamon)*, as explained by the phrase "because [I give you as] a father of a multitude of nations" (Gen. 17:5)

Abraham's wife, "Sarai" and "Sarah" are different forms of the same Hebrew word that basically means "princess/woman of strength". It is likely that Sarai is simply the possessive form of Sarah (i.e. "My Sarah"). Sarah, therefore, signifies that her strength does not belong exclusively to her immediate family, but to the future nation of Israel and even the world-at-large.

God made an agreement with Abram, a covenant that said he would be a great nation and God would bless him and he would be a blessing. And in him all the earth shall be blessed. (Gen.12: 1-3). This is interesting considering Abram was 75 years old with no offspring of his own. How could this be as Abram was 75 with no children? God is true to his word and he calls the things that we cannot see into existence. This is the law of faith. God saw it and spoke it and now he had to get Abram to see it and speak it.

Remember that in the first instance his name was Abram, exalted father but God had to change the mentality of Abram to Abraham, Father of a multitude of nations. To cause God's promise to be realised, God needed Abram to cooperate. God needed the internal image of Abram to change to Abraham.

As the story goes Abram moved from where he was into the land called Canaan.

Genesis 12: 7 God starts this image change by saying to Abram "*The Lord appeared to Abram and said, To your descendants I will give this land.*" Although Abram and Sarai had no offspring.

Here God is calling those things that be not as thought they were, These words that God spoke started something inside Abram. It started a new image of him being a Father of a multitude of nations. This is called Hope. For the next almost 25 years God worked with Abram to become Abraham. Examples are Genesis 13: 15-16 "*Descendants as the dust of the earth.*"

Genesis 15: 1 God shows himself as Adonai, his exceeding great reward. In verse 5 "*Look toward heaven and count the stars, if you are able to number them.......so shall your descendants be.*" All of these are changing the image inside Abram.

God changed Abrams name to Abraham, so every time his name was mentioned it was declaring—Father of a multitude of nations, This is calling things that be not as though they were.

For Abram to continue his transformation into Abraham, God called for the act of circumcision, a blood ratification of the covenant Abraham had with God, very personal relationship, imagine every time Abraham took a bath, changed his clothes, used the bathroom he saw a reminder of the promise of God. This was changing the inner image and therefore he was able to believe God. The end result is the promised was realised and the rest is history.

How did Abraham keep consistent for 25 years?

In his journey from Abram to Abraham he did make his share of mistakes, but Oh Ye perfect ones, who hasn't made any errors and we are born again with a new spirit,one that is exactly like Jesus, we have the Holy Spirit and many benefits as opposed to Abraham.

Lets take a wander to Romans 4: 16-22, here we see how Abraham maintained consistency.

It took a thing called discipline and right thinking.

"*(as it is written,"I have made you a father of many nations") in the presence of Him whom he believed—God, who gives life to the dead and calls those things which do not exist as though they did. who,* ***contrary to hope, in hope believed,*** *so that he became the father of many nations, according to what was spoken, "****So shall your descendants be."*** NKJV

And not being weak in faith, ***he did not consider his own body,*** *already dead (since he was about a hundred years old),and the deadness of Sarah's womb."*

To keep out doubt we need to follow the Example of Abraham. It says "***contrary to hope***."

Here Paul the witter of Romans is referring to natural Hope. Natural Hope or natural expectation. This is when you marry the hope of you and your spouse is you expect to have children. But for Abraham and Sarah this hope of having children disappeared many years before.

"In Hope Believed: So shall your dependants be" Through this Hope which came from the words spoken to Him from God he was able to believe, believe meaning trust, confidence, faith.

Through the images he saw in himself he was able to have faith. So Hope is a vital friend of Faith, they work together.

"And not being weak in faith, he did not consider his own body." In today's way of thinking ***not considering*** was Abraham's super power. This keeps doubt out.

He only considered, thought about, meditated on God's promise. This caused him to be fully convinced and not weak in faith. Being not weak in Faith brought the promise into physical manifestation. When you are fully convinced it is not difficult to believe the words you speak.

This is a great example for us to follow.

Jesus our great example

If we look at our greatest example of a life lived in Faith, the obvious choice is Jesus. If we look into how Jesus dealt with opportunity to doubt. In Luke 4: 1-13 we have great evidence and example on how to deal with contrary thoughts, Thoughts that are opposite to the truth of God's word. One thing the Bible does not say, that the devil appeared to Jesus but it says he was tempted by the devil. How was he tempted, through the avenue of thoughts.

This is exactly how we are tempted to doubt, Through suggested thoughts that are a manipulation of the truth, but not quite the truth. Some evidence on why I say this is found in Hebrews 4: 15 "*For we do not have a high priest who cannot sympathise with our weakness but was in all points tempted as we are yet without sin*". We are tempted through the manipulation of our thoughts. The book of James Chapter 1 talks about this.

I'm not saying that the devil didn't appear to Jesus, I'm simply saying in Luke 4 it only says he was tempted by the devil.

Lets us look at this perfect example.

Luke 4: 3-4 says, "*If you are the Son of God, command these stones to become bread.*" Notice the devil said "IF" and not "YOU ARE". The devil knows exactly who Jesus is but he starts with the element of doubt "IF". The same tactic was used against Adam and Eve in the garden.(Gen. 3: 1-6).

Jesus responded to the Fake question with the truth of the Word, verse 4: "*It is written, Man shall not live by bread alone but by every word of God.*" Oh, Ouch! That is an elbow to the devils solar plexus. (where the nerves of the stomach are located, often takes away the breath and is very painful.).

The devil tries again and takes him to a high mountain and shows him great things and suggests to Jesus that he, the devil can make him great and powerful, if only Jesus worships him.(Luke 4: 5-8). This is a little funny when you think about it because Jesus was already great and powerful, Jesus was and is the word, through him God created all things. (Col. 1: 16)

Again same tactic he used against Adam and Eve (Gen. 3: 5). "*For God knows that in the day you eat of it your eyes will be opened and you will be like God.....*" again a manipulation of thought because Adam and Eve were already like God (Gen. 1: 26-27).

Lets look at how Jesus responded. Luke 4: 8 says, "*And Jesus answered and said; Get behind me Satan "for it is written, You shall worship the Lord your God and him only shall you serve.*" NKJV

Oh perfect response, that is the punch to the throat of the devil.

The devil must be hurting, but one last attempt. The devil takes him to a high place, the pinnacle of the temple,(Luke 4: 9) a very high place and says, "*If you are the Son of God*" again the "IF" shows up, trying to put in the element of doubt. The devil tempts Jesus to prove who he is and throw himself to the ground. He manipulates the word of God to try and get Jesus to have incorrect thoughts about his outcome. (Luke 4: 10-11) But Jesus is not full of pride, he does not have to prove anything, especially to the devil, but he responded with the truth of the Word of God. "*And Jesus answered and said; It has been said, You shall not tempt the Lord your God.*" This is the final blow, it is the kick to the devils groin, the final piece of humiliation. The devil, departed beaten and bruised, Jesus dropped him to his knees and he crawled away totally beaten.

So it is with us when we are operating the Law of Faith, use these examples on how to keep the doubt from entering in to your heart.

Consider only the word said to you, meditate, ponder and think about the truth of the word. Don't let the "what If's" to stay in your thoughts. Don't allow the hypothetical to stay around your thoughts, a hypothetical is made up and are not a real scenario. Consider only the truth of God's word and speak that truth to the doubting thoughts and they will be defeated and depart.

Also notice how Jesus responded, He used the word to defeat the enemy but look at how skilful he was at the use of the word...the answered directly the temptation with the word, he did not answer with generic scripture but he answered the thought direct, with the perfect scripture.

We are to do the same, we are to become skilful in the use of the scriptures and the use of our words.

Chapter SIX

DO YOU BELIEVE WHAT YOU SAY?

What is 'to believe'? The Cambridge dictionary defines it as: *to think that something is true, correct and real.* Other synonyms: *trust, to be confident.*

Webster's 1828 dictionary says: *To expect or hope with confidence; to trust. To have a firm persuasion of any thing. In some cases, to have full persuasion, approaching to certainty;*

According to Jesus in Mark 11: 23-24 to be successful we must believe, trust, have confidence in and be fully persuaded in what we say. All else is idle words. Do we believe, trust, have confidence in and are fully persuaded that God hears us when we pray and that we already receive when we pray? If you are not fully persuaded, fix it, do what Abraham did in Romans 4. Consider only what God says, consider yours words.

Watch your words, if they are contrary to what you prayed then change them.

Integrity

Integrity has a vital part to play in using the law of faith. Integrity keeps the doubt away.

What is integrity? The state of being Honest and Upright.

Basically honour your word, do what you say you are going to do. If you say you will do something or be somewhere at a certain time, then be there or do the thing you say. It is very important, this is the way you believe what you say. If you are not constantly fulfilling your promises, your mind and your spirit will not believe you. But as you start to fulfil your promises to people, do what you say you will do, then you establish integrity in yourself and you start to believe you own words. So when you use the Law of Faith you will believe what you say. So keep your word.

The Bible talks about integrity Psalm 15: 4 "*...He honours who fear the Lord; He who swears to his own hurt and does not change*" He who honours his pledge.

Matthew 5: 37 says, "*But let your 'Yes' be 'Yes,' and your 'No,' 'No.' For whatever is more than these is from the evil one.*" Mean what you say. Be trustworthy. When you say 'Yes' mean 'Yes not maybe'. If you develop integrity with your words and action, when the critical times come, you will believe what you say.

Set your life's Direction

Your words are vitally important, they steer your ship. Your life sent in in the direction of your words. The book of James compares your words to a bit in a horses bridle, the bit in the bridle gives the horse direction. The same with the rudder on a ship. Just as a rudder gives the ship it's direction and sets it's course. So do your words. Your words sets the direction and course of your life. (James 3:1-5)

Change your words, change your life's direction. Believe your words and reap the result.

If we look at the of history of the exodus of the children of Israel. In the book of Numbers chapter 14, this shows clearly how powerful your words are and how we bind or release the power of God because of what we say.

This story starts in chapter 13, where Moses sent 12 spies to spy out the land of Canaan. 10 spies came back with a bad report and only two came back believing God at his word. Chapter 14 says the people believed the bad report.

So it is important not to believe the bad report, you have Gods word for it that he wants to prosper you (Jer. 29;11). Let your words echo Gods word.

If the congregation of Israelites believed God at his word their lives would be so different but they chose the '10 spies network of unbelief'.

Chapter SEVEN

BELIEVE YOU HAVE RECEIVED

*"Therefore I say to you, whatever things you ask when you pray, believe that you receive them, and you will have them".*NKJV

This verse can be broken into 4 parts.

1. ***"Therefore I say to you"*** This is Jesus speaking, we know from our previous look at the character of Jesus, He cannot lie, so we can be assured that he is telling the truth. We can draw confidence in what He is about to say.

2. ***"Whatever things you ask when you pray"*** From this we know that God wants us to ask of him and he also hears

us when we ask of him. Our communication (prayer) with God is a vital part of our daily walk with him. We are allowed to ask of him, he wants us to ask so that he can provide. Asking gives God permission to work on our behalf. One of the keys to asking is to ask according to His promises, God is a benevolent Father and it is his delight to give us the things we desire, but according to his will. Simply because his will is perfect for us and His will gives us exactly what we need when we need it, Proverbs 10:22 NKJV says, "*The blessing of the Lord makes one rich , and He adds no sorrow with it.*"

He won't give you next weeks Lottery numbers or the winner of race six at the race track. That requires no faith, it will bring sorrow. This type of "get the money quick" brings sorrow and takes your reliance on God away and you rely on the worlds system. God doesn't do "get rich quick".

Proverbs 13: 11 TPT says, "*Wealth quickly gained is quickly wasted.*"

Proverbs 13:11 NKJV says, "*Wealth gained by dishonesty will be diminished.*"

3. ***"Believe you receive when you pray"*** What is it to believe and what is it to receive? **If we remember the definition of " To Believe"**

The Cambridge dictionary defines it as: *to think that something is true, correct and real.* Other synonyms: *trust, to be confident.*

To "*believe you have received when you pray*" is to trust and be confident in what God has said. God cannot lie. He is full to overflowing with integrity. When He says something, he means it. No shadows, nothing slippery, no hidden agenda. Just the plain straight truth.

We know God shoots a straight arrow, when he says something: it is true, straight,correct and real.

So where is the receiving? According to Mark 11:24 the receiving is done before the "*you shall have*" before the actual manifestation. The receiving is done in the inner man prior to I have it as a tangible object.

If we look again at Abraham and the pattern he followed, God gave him a promise, he eventually received that promise inside himself. He started to call himself Abraham rather than Abram. He believed the promise, He spoke it out through saying his name. He saw himself as the Father of a multitude and he had the promise manifested. He made the promise of God his own.

Romans 4: 18 NKJV gives us insight into how Abraham received the promise and made it his own. "*Who* (Abraham)*contrary* (opposite)*to* (natural) *hope, in hope (*expectation of the promise spoken to him was true) *believed, so that he would become the father of many nations,according to what was spoken:'so shall your descendants be.'"*

Abraham took the Word of God and only considered it, he considered nothing else. This gave him hope and his faith had something to work with, it then became easy to receive because the promise was in him.

In 1 John 5: 14-15 NKJV "*This is the confidence we have in Him, that if we ask anything, according to his will, he hears us. And if we know he hears us, whatever we ask, we know we have the petitions that we have asked of Him."*

Be confident in him, know that he is for you and not against you. Be confident that He wants to supply your every need more than you want it supplied.

4. ***"And you shall have them"*** This is the manifestation, it is different from receiving. You shall have them is the result of receiving your inner man. In your inner being is where all things are produced.

One of the common terms in the Christian circles is "what are you believing for?" According to Mark11:23_24 the answer should be nothing. As I read Mark 11, according to the Law of faith that the term "believing" for something can be thought of as unbelief. Whatever you ask for when praying, know that God has heard you and he will respond because you believe you have it when you prayed. It is done when you pray. If you really believe you have it then it is easy to thank God for the supply. Our words should be "I have said therefore I have" or I prayed therefore I have."

In my understanding "believing" is for the future, it seems to indicate I receive, not now, but maybe later in the future. The Bible says "*believe you receive when you pray*" as I read and understand that statement the thing I pray for is already deposited within me, at the time I ask.

Meaning I have received it within my spirit, now, at the moment I pray. If I know that it has been deposited within me then I have received it I and therefore I have it. Regardless of how I feel or what I see.

Earlier in my walk with God I was a bit confused, and actually wondered if God hears me. The confusion came when I heard some preachers say that God doesn't hear your prays if you commit sin. I was sucked into this wrong way of thinking for awhile but after some time I realised a couple of things: I am not a sinner I am the righteous of God in Christ Jesus. (2 Cor. 5: 21.) God does not look at me through the flesh he looks at me through Jesus, through this righteousness, he looks at me as mature and whole.

Possibly the reason for delay in receiving my prayer is because I was double minded, asked for one thing then changed my mind. (James 1: 6-8) I did ask and believe I received but in truth I was a doubter, double minded. Simply because what I asked for was not in me, I didn't see it in my imagination. I asked it from mental assent and not from the solid foundation of what I saw inside me. On the occasion I did use what I saw in me, based on what God told me, it did manifest. It did turn out to be a great testimony.

I have a few personal testimonies that I could share but the one that comes to mind at the moment is how I received my motorcycle. I have always enjoyed motorcycles and have had many over the years, but one in particular is very special to me. I rode a lot in my younger days, in fact for many years I only owned a motorcycle and didn't own a car. I enjoyed riding so much. Move on a number of years and I got married and realised I had to become sensible and responsible so I sold my precious machines and the parts I had to another enthusiast. Yes my beautiful 1939 side valve Harley with foot clutch and tractor seat. Insert crying face here. I was determined to be a responsible husband and eventually father, but motorcycles were inside me and still are.

Many years later, I was involved with a christian motorcycle ministry, yet I had a problem, yes your right….no motorcycle.

I did what I knew to do, I prayed and asked for a motorcycle. One day I was cleaning up my garage and In that quiet time alone, God spoke to me and said, "*it's time you believed me for a motorcycle*" my response was "I want more than one" and of course God being God said to me, "yes I know, how many?" I have wondered over the years why God asked "how many?" He knew. It is because he wanted me to tell him, to give him permission to act on my behalf. So I told him and I was very specific in what I wanted. I gave God the details. How I did this was by using the principles of hope and faith. I researched the bikes and got a picture inside me of the ones I wanted and petitioned God.

A number of years later, yes I said 'years', I was at home and I received an unexpected phone call from a business man I knew. He said to me "I was about to go into a meeting to sign a million dollar contract but God stopped me and said, "you have to buy Maurice the motorcycle of his choice today." That caused him to call me. We went to the Harley Davidson distributor of the day and I asked for a Road King Classic. At that time in my country you had to order your bike and it would come in the next shipment from the USA. The salesman went to check his stock sheet, and to his amazement he had one in stock, in the crate, in the warehouse.

Apparently someone had ordered it and rang that morning and cancelled the order. That bike was mine from the moment I saw it in me and when it was being manufactured in the assembly line, it was mine. This is one of many things that God has done for me, and it is one of many reasons why I know this principle works for whoever will make a decision to use the Law of Faith.

One scripture that really made me realise that God always hears a believer is found in John 11: 41-41, "....*Then they took away the stone from the place where the dead man was lying. And Jesus lifted up His eyes and said, "Father, I thank You that You have heard Me. And I know that You always hear Me, but because of the people who are standing by I said this, that they may believe that You sent Me."*

When I read this I realised that God always hears Jesus. If God hears Jesus every time, then he hears me every time. "*This is the confidence that we have in him that if we ask anything according to his will, he hears us" (1John 5: 14)And if we know that he hears us, whatever we ask we know that we have the petitions that we have asked of him." (1John 5:15)*

Also we can read in Psalm 91: 15 TPT, ***"I WILL Answer*** *your pray for help* ***every time*** *you pray."* Have confidence in these words.

That sounds very definitive to me. So now we can confidently use Mark 11: 24.

Chapter EIGHT

FAITH WORKS BY LOVE

"*And whenever you stand praying, if you have anything against anyone, forgive him, that your Father in heaven may also forgive you your trespasses. But if you do not forgive, neither will your Father in heaven forgive your trespasses.*" NKJV

Please note this scripture doesn't say God doesn't hear you, it says to walk in love you need to forgive, unforgiveness is darkness.

It doesn't matter how dynamic Faith is or how creative and important your imagination is, or how important Hope is to Faith. Everything in the Kingdom of God works by Love. Love being the unconditional Love. This is God Himself. 1 John 4: 8 "*God is Love*".

As I understand things, one of the indicators that you are operating in Love is your willingness and ability to forgive. The Love that is in you is Gods Love or God himself. Human love fades and can end but this Love we are to walk in is Gods love.

Look at the explanation Jesus gave regarding forgiveness. Matthew 18: 21-25 "*Then Peter came to Him and said, "Lord, how often shall my brother sin against me, and I forgive him? Up to seven times?"*

Jesus went on to explain the importance of forgiveness.

Jesus said to him, "I do not say to you, up to seven times, but up to seventy times seven. Therefore the kingdom of heaven is like a certain king who wanted to settle accounts with his servants. And when he had begun to settle accounts, one was brought to him who owed him ten thousand talents. But as he was not able to pay, his master commanded that he be sold, with his wife and children and all that he had, and that payment be made. The servant therefore fell down before him, saying, 'Master, have patience with me, and I will pay you all.' Then the master of that servant was moved with compassion, released him, and forgave him the debt.

"But that servant went out and found one of his fellow servants who owed him a hundred denarii; and he laid hands on him and took him by the throat, saying, 'Pay me what you owe!' So his fellow servant fell down at his feet and begged him, saying, 'Have patience with me, and I will pay you all.' And he would not, but went and threw him into prison till he should pay the debt. So when his fellow servants saw what had been done, they were very grieved, and came and told their master all that had been done. Then his master, after he had called him, said to him, 'You wicked servant! I forgave you all that debt because you begged me. Should you not also have had compassion on your fellow servant, just as I had pity on you?' And his master was angry, and delivered him to the torturers until he should pay all that was due to him. NKJV

"So My heavenly Father also will do to you if each of you, from his heart, does not forgive his brother his trespasses."

This a great story of a man who was totally forgiven of all debt. This is exactly what has happened to the ones who believe on Jesus Christ, 100% forgiven of all trespasses.

We notice in this teaching that the man obviously did not understand what a great thing forgiveness of his debt is. In him there was no understanding of forgiveness. He went about very ruthless and selfishly demanded that none of his debtors be forgiven. Even though he himself was totally forgiven. The light of forgiveness shone on this man he himself did not recognise it and was still full of darkness and the end result for that man was not good.

In the first epistle (a letter) of John he talks about unforgiveness and that those who do not have forgiveness toward others, especially fellow believers, they live in darkness.

1 John 2: 9- 11 "*He who says he is in the light, and hates his brother, is in darkness until now. He who loves his brother abides in the light, and there is no cause for stumbling in him. But he who hates his brother is in darkness and walks in darkness, and does not know where he is going, because the darkness has blinded his eyes.*" NKJV

To forgive is to walk in the light, to forgive expels any darkness in you.

Where is this darkness kept? I believe it is in your soul realm, I don't believe it is in the spirit of the born again believer, simply because your spirit is completely new and has the same character nature of God and is in right standing with God. It is also sealed with the Holy Spirit.

Unforgiveness causes hatred, bitterness, anger and opens the door for the enemy to control your life. Unforgiveness allows the works of the flesh to dominate you, and we know in the book of Galatians that the work of the flesh is in opposition to the Spirit.

Forgiveness is a choice. Walk in light or walk in darkness...your choice.

Forgiveness is not a sign of weakness but a sign of true strength and character.

To forgive is a mighty powerful weapon, it is an act of Love. Unconditional love is not soft or gooey, it is a mighty and powerful force, it is what caused Jesus to die on the cross. That is not soft.

Forgiveness is a true sign of Love. Look at what God did for us, His willingness to forgive mankind after the treachery we showed him, When we look at what God has done, it's easy to see unconditional Love in practice. When Jesus says, "*if you have anything against anyone, forgive him.*" He is saying walk in the love, forgive, the light is in you and you will not walk in the darkness, you will not block anything God is trying to do for you. As much as God wants to bless you and those blessings are real and available, you are not able to receive them while walking in the darkness of unforgiveness and hate. Unforgiveness and hate does not align you with God. It is not who you really are. You are the children of light and love. You are not weighed down heaviness of unforgiveness or hate. Take that care and give it to God, that heaviness does not belong in any of us. But the peace of God does belong to us.

Love is an amazing thing, when I say love I mean Agape, unconditional love. This is God himself. It is this great attribute that caused God to put in place his great reset. God chose to reset man's ability to have fellowship and communion with him. Just as we saw in the story of the prodigal son. (Luke 15)

This love is what caused God to forgive mankind and reinstate us as his sons/daughters. Obviously the doorway to this greatness is to believe on Jesus the Christ. The whole world is forgiven but not all accept Christ as saviour. The power of Jesus's blood cleansed everything.

In 1 Corinthians 13: 1- 13 this scripture gives us an inside view of Love's character and therefore God's character. It tells us that Love (God) is patient, not envious, does not show off to attract attention, it is not arrogant, is not rude, nor seeks its own (not selfish), is not provoked (is very secure in its self), doesn't think evil (only thinks good). Only rejoices in the truth, bears, believes, hopes and endures all things. This love never fails. God never fails.

These are great attributes. The Bible says in Galatians 5: 12 that love is a fruit or product of the spirit. This is what your new spirit looks like, so it is already in you. It is ready to forgive, in fact this love in you wants to forgive. At times we hold back showing the world the goodness of God, through unforgiveness.

The Bible also says that "*the love of God has been poured out in our hearts by the Holy Spirit, who is given to us.*" Romans 5: 5.

We can plainly see that the capacity to walk in love and forgive is in us, it is our opportunity to show the world God himself.

Note: if you are starting to feel unwell or have a bad diagnosis from the doctor, remember the word says by '*His stripes you WERE healed*' (1 Peter 2: 24) but also remember that '*Faith works by Love*' (Gal. 5:6).

In other words if illness comes upon you ask the Holy Spirit for remembrance of any unforgiveness or weight you might be carrying. When he reveals it act quickly to fix it.

GOD IN ACTION

The story of the prodigal son in Luke 15:11-32 Shows a great example of God's love for man and how he treats his creation. The meaning of prodigal is to be a wasteful, unwise, reckless with your resources.

The story of the prodigal son has a few different angles to it. This story tells us of how God views his creation, how he views people and his Love for people. It is the story of mankind and his relationship with God, it is also a story of individual people who do stray a way from God. But mostly it is a story of God's love for mankind as a whole as well as individually. It is also an explanation for the faithful believer who stayed with God through everything.

"Then He said: "A certain man had two sons. And the younger of them said to his father, 'Father, give me the portion of goods that falls to me.' So he divided to them his livelihood. And not many days after, the younger son gathered all together, journeyed to a far country, and there wasted his possessions with prodigal living. But when he had spent all, there arose a severe famine in that land, and he began to be in want.

Then he went and joined himself to a citizen of that country, and he sent him into his fields to feed swine. And he would gladly have filled his stomach with the pods that the swine ate, and no one gave him anything.

"But when he came to himself, he said, 'How many of my father's hired servants have bread enough and to spare, and I perish with hunger! I will arise and go to my father, and will say to him, "Father,I have sinned against heaven and before you, and I am no longer worthy to be called your son. Make me like one of your hired servants."

"And he arose and came to his father. But when he was still a great way off, his father saw him and had compassion, and ran and fell on his neck and kissed him. And the son said to him, 'Father, I have

sinned against heaven and in your sight, and am no longer worthy to be called your son.'

"But the father said to his servants, 'Bring out the best robe and put it on him, and put a ring on his hand and sandals on his feet. And bring the fatted calf here and kill it, and let us eat and be merry; for this my son was dead and is alive again; he was lost and is found.' And they began to be merry.

"Now his older son was in the field. And as he came and drew near to the house, he heard music and dancing. So he called one of the servants and asked what these things meant. And he said to him, 'Your brother has come, and because he has received him safe and sound, your father has killed the fatted calf.'

"But he was angry and would not go in. Therefore his father came out and pleaded with him. So he answered and said to his father, 'Lo, these many years I have been serving you; I never transgressed your commandment at any time; and yet you never gave me a young goat, that I might make merry with my friends. But as soon as this son of yours came, who has devoured your livelihood with harlots, you killed the fatted calf for him.'

"And he said to him, 'Son, you are always with me, and all that I have is yours. It was right that we should make merry and be glad, or your brother was dead and is alive again, and was lost and is found.'"

This is a great story of God's attitude towards mankind. In the beginning God created man in his image and likeness (Gen.1: 26), But through some very bad decisions, man went his own way and became wasteful, reckless and unwise with what God had given him. He became lost and a prodigal. God in his great and infinite Love, Grace, Mercy and Wisdom made a way for man to return to him. To continue the father- child relationship that they both wanted.

When man realised his stupidity and said "what am I doing with my life, there is only destruction that lays ahead of me if I continue this lifestyle." He found his way back to the Father. The next thing that the Father did is very important, notice the Father did not rebuke the son, he didn't call him a loser or wasteful, unwise fool. No instead he ran towards the son and embraced him and loved him. The Father made a big deal and celebrated the return of his son. The Father bestowed upon the son all the rightful things that originally owned and was his.

So to God does the same for us, now in this time He loves on anyone who finds their way back to him, through Jesus Christ. God Loves on that person, God bestows everything that is rightfully theirs from the beginning of creation.

God does not hate you, God does not own a big stick to beat you with. He is Love.

As you can see you do not have to work your way back into God's love, it is always there. The son thought he could work his way back into the Fathers love, he saw himself as a wasteful, unwise man, and was prepared to be a servant but the Father saw him as a son.

This is how God sees you, a son/daughter, through the great act of Love and forgiveness manifested through Christ

See yourself as God sees you. You are not a low life scum, you have a Father that adores you and eagerly awaits your return to him. He wants to restore all things to you.

If Religion tells you different, it seems that religion hasn't read the Bible.

The other important thing to notice here is the issue that the older brother has and the Fathers response.

"Now his older son was in the field. And as he came and drew near to the house, he heard music and dancing. So he called one of the servants and asked what these things meant. And he said to him, 'Your brother has come, and because he has received him safe and sound, your father has killed the fatted calf.'

"But he was angry and would not go in. Therefore his father came out and pleaded with him. So he answered and said to his father, 'Lo, these many years I have been serving you; I never transgressed your commandment at any time; and yet you never gave me a young goat, that I might make merry with my friends. But as soon as this son of yours came, who has devoured your livelihood with harlots, you killed the fatted calf for him.'

*"And he said to him, '**Son, you are always with me, and all that I have is yours**. It was right that we should make merry and be glad, for your brother was dead and is alive again, and was lost and is found.'"*

We as born again believers, it is import that we realise we already have and always had everything that God has. We have full access to all of God's stuff. Don't sell yourself short, God says here "ALL I have is YOURS". Folks, it's ours already, it's ours to access now.

We access everything through the Law of Faith.

PRAYER OF SALVATION

This is a prayer where we confess to God our need for him and our need to receive Jesus Christ in our hearts to be our Lord. This prayer is heart felt and confessed with the mouth.

Heavenly Father, I come to You in the Name of Jesus. Your Word says, "Whosoever shall call on the name of the Lord shall be saved" (***Acts 2:21***)*. I am calling on You. I pray and ask Jesus to come into my heart and be Lord over my life according to* ***Romans 10:9-10****: "If thou shalt confess with thy mouth the Lord Jesus, and shalt believe in thine heart that God has raised him from the dead, thou shalt be saved. For with the heart man believeth unto righteousness; and with the mouth* *confession is made unto salvation." I do that now. I confess that Jesus is Lord, and I believe in my heart that God raised Him from the dead.*

I am now reborn! I am a Christian—a child of Almighty God! I am saved!

PRAYER TO RECEIVE THE HOLY SPIRIT

*You said in Your Word, "If ye then being evil, know how to give good gifts unto your children: HOW MUCH MORE shall your heavenly Father give the Holy Spirit to them that ask him?" (**Luke 11:13**). I'm also asking You to fill me with the Holy Spirit. Holy Spirit, rise up within me as I praise God. I fully expect to speak with other tongues as You give me the utterance (**Acts 2:4**). In Jesus' Name. Amen.*

REFERENCES

King James Bible https://biblehub.com/

New King James Bible https://biblehub.com/

Amplified Bible https://biblehub.com/

The Literal Standard Version ttps://biblehub.com/mark/11-22.htm

Berean Literal Bible https://biblehub.com/

Young's Literal translation ttps://biblehub.com/mark/11-22.htm
Smith's Literal translation ttps://biblehub.com/mark/11-22.htm
The Passion Translation

The Bible Hub https://biblehub.com

Strong's Concordance https://biblehub.com/strongs.htm

Kenneth Copeland Ministries prayer for Salvation

Kenneth Copeland Ministries prayer to receive the Holy Spirit
Cambridge Dictionary https://dictionary.cambridge.org/

Websters 1828 Dictionary https://webstersdictionary1828.com

Dr. Eli Lizorkin-Eyzenberg and Rev. Jim Stowe
https://weekly.israelbiblecenter.com/the-meaning-of-the-hebrew-names

Vines Expository Dictionary

www.ingramcontent.com/pod-product-compliance
Lightning Source LLC
LaVergne TN
LVHW020648100826
845148LV00012B/2378

* 9 7 8 1 7 6 4 5 6 2 0 3 4 *